Published 1979 by Warwick Press Inc., 730 Fifth Avenue,
New York, New York 10019.

First published in Great Britain by Angus and Robertson
(U.K.) Ltd., 1979.

Printed in Hong Kong by Mandarin Publishers Ltd.

Library of Congress Catalog Card No. 78-63099
ISBN 0-531-09099-X
ISBN 0-531-09109-0 lib. bdg.

# The Otter

By Angela Sheehan
Illustrated by Bernard Robinson

WARWICK PRESS · NEW YORK

With one slight, swift movement, the otter slipped into the water. She made no noise and her sleek body hardly disturbed the still surface of the pool. Only a few ripples lapped their way to the muddy bank. Then all was calm, until the same thin ripples spread out again a short distance away, and the otter surfaced. As the animal swam to the bank, the moonlight caught the silvery scales of the fish she gripped in her mouth. But the otter did not linger in the light. She slid into the shelter of the reeds and ate her tasty meal.

When she had finished the fish, the otter set off along the river bank. By morning light, she was far from the hole where she had spent the day before. But she had no need to return to that hole. There were plenty more places where she could rest.

As soon as she found a hole, the otter pushed her way in. The moss-lined tunnel was dark and narrow. The entrance was so small that it squeezed the water out of her furry coat.

All day she slept in the hole. No light reached her, but she had plenty of air. The otter that had dug the hole in the first place had made a shaft to the surface to let in air.

All through the fall, she spent the daytime curled up in a hole. At night she wandered along the river, finding fishes, frogs and insects to eat.

Soon the reeds by the water's edge turned brown. The leaves fell from the trees that grew along the bank. Winter had come.

When the river froze, the otter had to swim under the ice to catch her food. It was hard work for her. She could only swim a little way before running out of air. Then she had to hurry back to the breathing hole she had made in the ice. Night after night, the ice on the river grew thicker. It was time for her to find a better stretch of water.

The otter set off early in the evening.
She crossed one snowy field after another.
By dawn, she had reached the top of a high
hill, and she could see a broad river below
her. It was still flowing. The otter ran as fast
as she could towards it.

At the top of the bank, she stopped, sank to her stomach, and launched herself over the edge. Down she went, down the steep, slippery slope, faster and faster. At the bottom she came to a halt, panting. She rested for a moment, then stretched herself ready to plunge into the river. But she did not plunge. Instead, she turned, raced back up the slope and slid all the way down again. Time and again the otter launched herself down the slide.

By the time she stopped her games, the otter was too tired to swim or catch fish. She wanted only to sleep. So she found a hollow in some bushes on the bank and soon fell fast asleep.

That evening she woke, hungry and stiff. Again she slid down the slope, but this time she did not run back again. She plunged into the river. Soon she came upon some eels, her favorite food. She caught the wriggling creatures, one after another, dragging them from the water with her sharp teeth.

Night after night, she traveled farther downstream. The river grew wider and wider. The banks of the river soon disappeared altogether. The otter had reached the sea. It was morning and time to find a hiding place. But there were no otter holes on the shore. So she braved the daylight in the water. She swam in the shallows, twisting and rolling about.

Later in the day, she rested among the tangled seaweeds on the rocks. Then, watched by a crowd of birds, she caught some food : shrimps and mussels and lots of little fishes. Everything was new.

After a few days, the otter had still not found a good place to sleep. The sea made her feel tired, and she longed to drink fresh river water again. So she left the sea and made her way upstream.

Robinson

Before long the mud flats by the river gave way to tree-lined banks. And the otter was able to spend her third day upstream snug among the roots of a tree. She did not know that a male otter was sleeping close by. In the evening the two otters left their hiding places at the same time. They chased the same fish and watched each other as they swam. They raced each other to catch a duck. The female chased the male, and he chased her. They were so busy with their games that they hardly ate at all.

By daybreak, they had moved even farther upstream. There the two stayed. At night, they caught birds, frogs and fish. They often played together in the water or on the bank. During the day, they each found a hole to sleep in ; and if they could not find one, they dug one.

One night, the two otters noticed some fine big salmon swimming upstream. They each raced after one of them. The male snatched at his first, but he only managed to grip a fin in his mouth. The fish wrenched its body away and swam off. The female sank her sharp teeth into the body of her salmon and held on to it. She dragged her prize from the water and settled down to eat it.

While the otter ate the salmon, the male watched from the other side of the river. Then he swam across and crept towards her. She was too busy to see him or hear his light tread. He waited, making a soft squeaking noise. The female heard the noise and greeted the male by squeaking back to him. He edged forward and bit into the salmon.

By now, she had eaten quite enough, so she went for a swim while the male ate. Even he could not finish the fish. Its half-eaten body lay on the bank as he took to the water. His playmate greeted him and they swam lazily together. They did not go straight to their burrows that morning. Instead they played for a while and then mated.

Six weeks later, the female left the river.
She climbed the bank and searched for a
place to dig her burrow. Her mate stayed by
the river, but still saw her as she came and
went to her new home. One night, she did not
come to the river. She stayed in the burrow.
The time had come to give birth to her cubs.

Deep in the warm burrow, the tiny blind cubs snuggled up to their mother. They sucked milk from her body and slept all day and all night. Their father never saw them. But sometimes he brought a frog or a fish to the mouth of the burrow for his mate to eat. It was hungry work for her, feeding the cubs and having little to eat herself.

It was two whole months before the tiny cubs made their way to the entrance. Their mother urged them on but they were too scared to go far. They were also too scared to be left behind when she went off to fish. So in the end they had to follow her. Every sight, sound and smell was strange. But they enjoyed running along behind their mother.

But as soon as they came to the water's edge they stopped. The waves lapped over their feet and made them cold and wet. Their mother dived in but the three youngsters stayed on the bank, huddled together. So she climbed out of the water and gently pushed them down to the brink. Suddenly one of the cubs lost his footing and tumbled into the water.

He clutched wildly at a waterplant and squeaked with fear but nothing could save him now. He was in the water. But it was not so frightening after all; in fact, it felt warm and smooth, and he could swim. Slowly, the other two cubs followed him.

Once all three were in the water, they had a fine time, diving, splashing and plunging. They swam along behind their mother and jumped on her back for a ride.

The otter cubs loved the water, but they could not stay there all the time. They explored the fields. They ate insects and slugs and worms and frogs.

The cubs never saw their father. Their mother no longer needed him, so he made his way downstream. Next year he would find a new mate, and so would she.

During the winter, the rest of the family snuggled up in a new burrow nearer the river. One windy evening, just as they were about to leave the burrow, they heard a loud groaning noise. The ground seemed to shudder. Suddenly a great tree root ripped through the wall of the burrow. An old willow tree had been uprooted by the gale. The animals struggled through the falling earth to get clear of the root.

The two female cubs whimpered at their mother's side. The young male cub was nowhere to be seen. He had been at the very end of the tunnel and was now cut off. Outside, soil and stones were hailing down the slope. The three otters headed for the water and swam as fast and as far as they could.

It was a long time before the fallen tree came to rest. The young otter, buried alive far below the surface, waited in terror. Soon there was silence and stillness. The little otter scratched above his head and saw a tiny beam of light. The shaft his mother had made to let in air had held firm. The otter tried to widen the narrow tube. He worked slowly, scraping the soil with his paws.

After several hours, his body felt stiff and his paws were sore. But he was free and alive. The others were far away. He would never see them again. He swam to the far bank of the river, and slept curled up under a tree.

That same night, the otter and the two female cubs left the river and made their way overland to a small pool. Throughout the winter they stayed together helping each other to find food and shelter.

With spring the warm weather came. The otter wandered far from the pool. She often went to the big river where the eels were again making their way upstream. The young females liked to find holes for themselves now. They, too, wandered far.

The otter's family had gone for good now. Soon it would be time for her to find another mate and rear another family. The young females, too, would be ready to mate, and so would their brother, far, far away.

# More About Otters

**Eyes** on top of head so the otter can see above the water

**Ears** which can be sealed underwater

**Tail** long and flexible for use as a rudder

**Nose** high up so the otter can breathe while swimming

**Whiskers** long and sensitive to vibrations in the water.

**Teeth** strong and sharp for holding and biting flesh and cracking shellfish

**Back feet** webbed for paddling

**Front feet** with claws for digging

**The body of the common otter**

The name of the otter in the story is the common otter. It lives in the United States and Canada, and in Europe, parts of Asia and the northern tip of Africa.

## Acrobats in the Water

The otter is perfectly suited for its life in the water. Its eyes have special lenses so that it can see clearly underwater. When the water is too murky, the otter can feel its way with its long whiskers. Its eyes and nostrils are high on its head so it can see above the surface of the water and breathe without lifting its head above the surface.

The otter's slim body and flat head allow it to slip easily through the water. When it swims on the surface of the water it paddles with its powerful webbed back feet. Swimming underwater it draws its leg into its body and moves by wriggling its tail and body like an eel. It uses its tail as a rudder.

## Night Prowlers

Fish and other small water animals are the otter's main food. It usually feeds at night and is a swift, cunning hunter. One of its tricks is to swim up behind a fish so that the fish cannot see it. Otters have

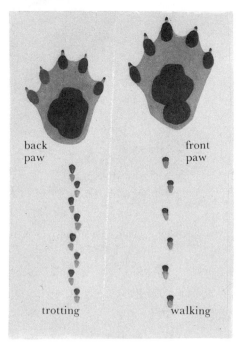

back
paw

front
paw

trotting            walking

**If you see any of these tracks by a river, watch carefully and quietly and you may be lucky enough to see an otter.**

small clawed otter of India and Asia, the clawless otter of Africa and the giant Brazilian otter are very rare indeed.

The sea otter in the picture is shorter and fatter than river otters. It lives, breeds and eats in the sea. It even sleeps in the sea. wrapping seaweed around its body to stop it from floating away. When it eats, it floats on its back and uses its belly as a table. It breaks open the shellfish it likes by smashing them with a stone.

been known to swim underneath ducks and pull them underwater. Even out of the water they are skillful hunters, catching and eating small rodents.

### Otters in Danger
Otters are hunted for their fur, especially, in cold northern regions where the fur grows thicker. Because of this, even the well known types of otter are hard to find now. Other types, such as the